WITHDRAWN

SKATEBOARDING

How It Works

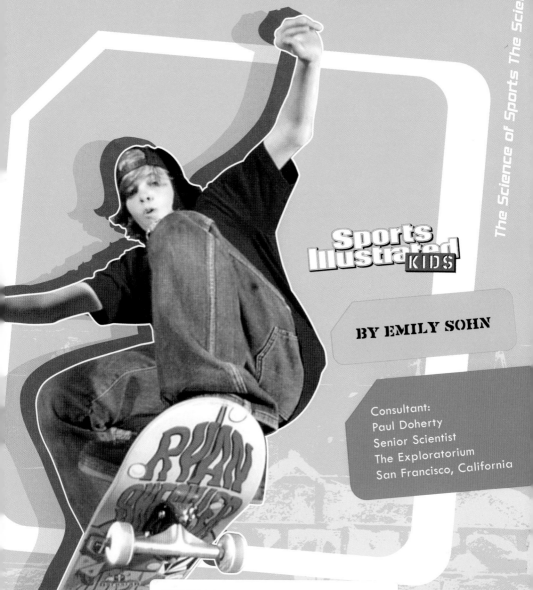

Sports Illustrated KIDS

BY EMILY SOHN

Consultant:
Paul Doherty
Senior Scientist
The Exploratorium
San Francisco, California

WEST PALM BEACH PUBLIC LIBRARY
411 CLEMATIS STREET
WEST PALM BEACH , FL 33401
(561) 868-7700

CAPSTONE PRESS
a capstone imprint

Sports Illustrated KIDS The Science of Sports is published by Capstone Press,
151 Good Counsel Drive, P.O. Box 669, Mankato, Minnesota 56002.
www.capstonepress.com

Copyright © 2010 by Capstone Press, a Capstone imprint. All rights reserved.
No part of this publication may be reproduced in whole or in part, or stored in a
retrieval system, or transmitted in any form or by any means, electronic, mechanical, photocopying,
recording, or otherwise, without written permission of the publisher or, where applicable, Time Inc.
For information regarding permission, write to Capstone Press,
151 Good Counsel Drive, P.O. Box 669, Dept. R, Mankato, Minnesota 56002.

Sports Illustrated Kids is a trademark of Time Inc. Used with permission.
Printed in the United States of America in Melrose Park, Illinois.

092009
005620LKS10

Books published by Capstone Press are manufactured with paper
containing at least 10 percent post-consumer waste.

Library of Congress Cataloging-in-Publication Data
Sohn, Emily.
   Skateboarding: how it works / by Emily Sohn.
   p. cm. — (Sports Illustrated KIDS. The Science of Sports)
   Includes bibliographical references and index.
   Summary: "Describes the science behind the sport of skateboarding, including basic skills, tricks,
skateparks, and competitions" — Provided by publisher.
   ISBN 978-1-4296-4024-4 (library binding)
   ISBN 978-1-4296-4877-6 (paperback)
1. Skateboarding — Juvenile literature. I. Title. II. Series.
GV859.8.S6 2010
796.22 — dc22   2009032783

Editorial Credits
Mandy Robbins, editor; Ted Williams, designer; Jo Miller, media researcher;
   Eric Manske, production specialist

Design Element Credits
Shutterstock/Eray Haciosmanoglu; kamphi

Photo Credits
Alamy/david sanger photography, 41 (inset); Frances Roberts,
   21 (inset); Kevin Foy, 30–31 (bottom); Ladi Kim, 24–25; MEB_Photography, 20–21;
   Stephen Harrison, 18–19; WorldFoto, 40–41
Capstone Studio/Gary Sundermeyer, 8 (inset wheel); Karon Dubke, 6 (both)
Dreamstime/Fritzkocher, 31 (top)
Getty Images Inc./Cameron Spencer, 10–11; Chris Polk, 22–23; Christian Petersen, 38 (top), 43;
   Christian Pondella, 44 (both); Doug Pensinger, 32–33; Elsa, 15 (inset); Harry How, 34–35;
   Jeff Gross, 14–15; Jonathan Moore, cover (main photo); LatinContent/Julio Cesar Guimaraes, 13;
   Victor Decolongon, 4–5; WireImage/Phillip Ellsworth, 45 (main image)
iStockphoto/homegrowngraphics, cover (wheel); Kevin Russ, 33 (inset); Pgiam, 30 (top)
Lily Rodriguez, (c) Exploratorium, www.exploratorium.edu, 26–27 (all)
Newscom/Icon/SMI/Tony Donaldson, 28, 29 (both)
Shutterstock/ ImageryMajestic, 7; M. Dykstra, 8–9; Steven Paul Pepper, cover (graffiti); terekhov igor,
   23 (inset); Timothy Lee Lantgen, cover (skateboard park rail); Vladimir Ivanovich Danilov,
   cover (bottom center)
Sports Illustrated/Robert Beck, cover (bottom right), cover (bottom left), 1, 3, 5 (inset), 16, 17,
   38 (bottom), 42, 45 (inset)
Zuma Press/Cal Sport Media/John C. Middlebrook, 36–37; Quiksilver/DC/Mike Blabac 39

TABLE OF CONTENTS

SKATEBOARDING: WHERE SCIENCE MEETS FUN

One piece of wood, two metal **TRUCKS**, and four wheels. A skateboard looks like such a simple object. Yet, experienced skaters can do amazing tricks. They jump. They spin. They flip. Then they land on their feet and keep cruising. It almost seems like magic.

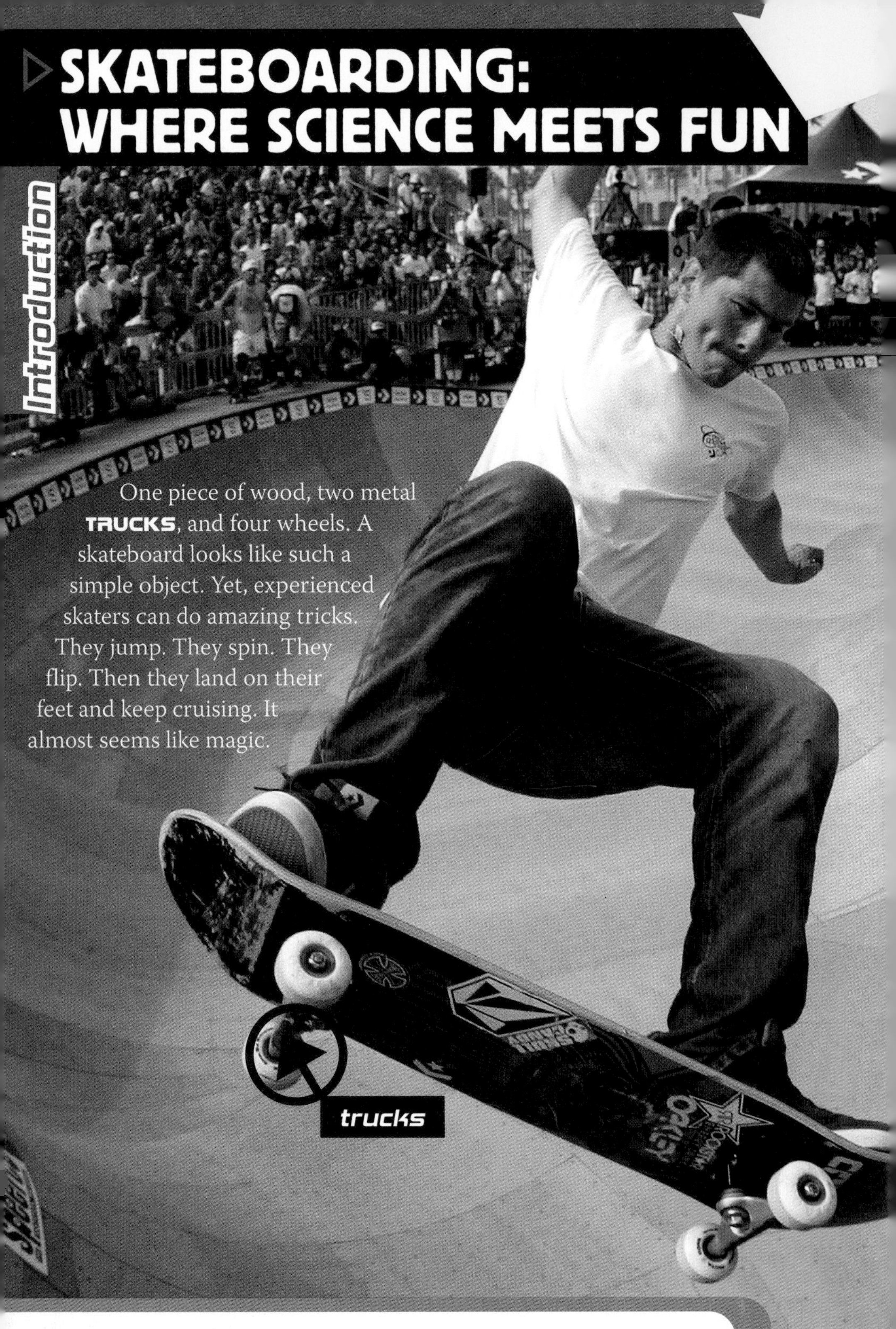

trucks

4

TRUCKS — the parts of a skateboard that attach the wheels to the deck

Every skateboarding skill is an example of science in action. There's physics behind the shape of the board and the size of the wheels. Biology explains the way a skater moves his shoulders and bends his knees. And that's just the beginning.

Even when you understand how it works, it's tough to pull off a successful Ollie, 360, or rail slide. Skillful skateboarding requires a lot of practice and a dose of creativity.

gravity
The skater fights gravity when doing aerial tricks.

There are two main types of skateboards: shortboards and longboards. Longboards are perfect for cruising and carving big, smooth turns. Shortboards are better for doing tricks. They are lightweight and compact, making them easier to move and get off the ground.

shortboard
7 to 8 inches (18 to 20 centimeters) wide
30 to 32 inches (76 to 81 centimeters) long

longboard
about 12 inches (30 centimers) wide
30 to 40 inches (76 to 102 centimeters) long

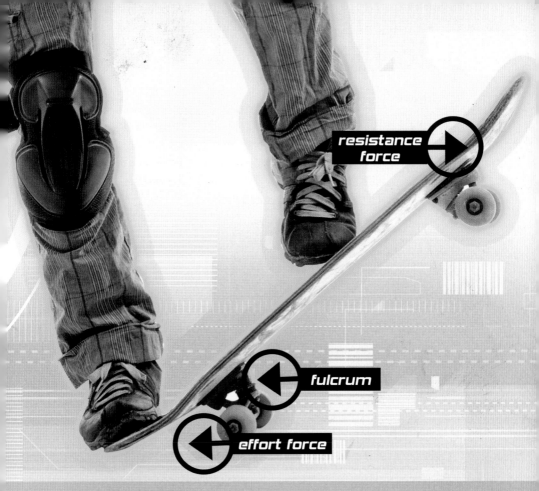

resistance force

fulcrum

effort force

A skateboard is a kind of simple machine called a first-class lever. This type of lever acts sort of like a seesaw. The wheels and trucks are **FULCRUMS**, also called pivot points. Each fulcrum lies between two forces: the effort force and the resistance force. Pushing down on the kicktail just a small amount makes the front of the board rise a lot.

NEWTON'S THIRD LAW OF MOTION:

For every action there is an equal and opposite reaction. As you cruise along, your weight and the weight of your skateboard push down on the surface below. This surface pushes back with an equal and opposite force.

FULCRUM — a resting point where a lever bar turns

Without wheels, a skateboard is just a plank of wood. Skateboard wheels range from 2 inches (5 centimeters) to 4 inches (10 centimeters) in **DIAMETER**. They can be hard or soft, thick or thin, and they come in many different colors.

diameter

Skaters who use longboards like their wheels big and soft. Large, soft wheels help absorb the impact of cracks and bumps in pavement. These wheels cruise smoothly on rough streets. A smaller, harder wheel provides a slower, bumpier ride.

DIAMETER — the distance from one side of a circle to the opposite side through the center

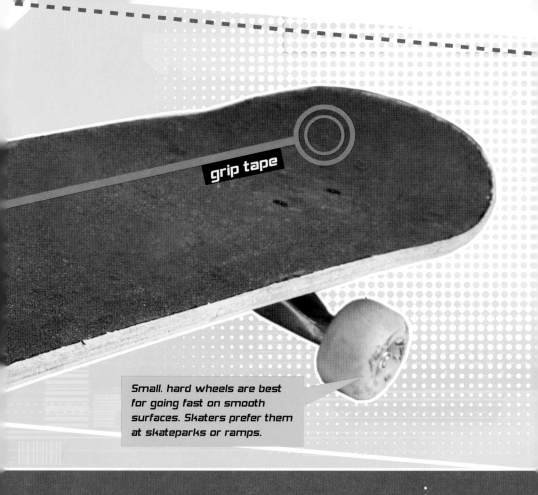

grip tape

Small. hard wheels are best for going fast on smooth surfaces. Skaters prefer them at skateparks or ramps.

FRICTION

To keep from sliding off the board, skaters apply grip tape to the deck. The bottom of the tape is sticky. The top is rough like sandpaper. The secret to grip tape is FRICTION.

Smooth objects have less friction than rough objects. Skaters experience two types of friction. Sliding friction has to do with the skater's feet rubbing against the board. Skaters use grip tape to increase friction and help their feet grip the board.

Rolling friction has to do with the wheels rolling against the ground. As a wheel rotates, the bottom flattens against the ground. When it rotates away from the ground, it springs back to its circular shape again. All this friction creates heat. Feel a skateboard's wheels right after a tough session. They'll be hot!

FRICTION — a force created when two objects rub together; friction slows down objects.

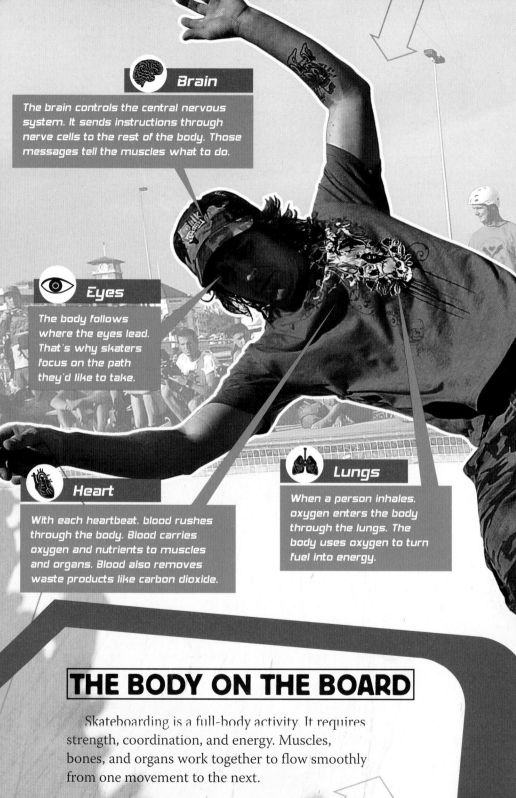

Brain

The brain controls the central nervous system. It sends instructions through nerve cells to the rest of the body. Those messages tell the muscles what to do.

Eyes

The body follows where the eyes lead. That's why skaters focus on the path they'd like to take.

Heart

With each heartbeat, blood rushes through the body. Blood carries oxygen and nutrients to muscles and organs. Blood also removes waste products like carbon dioxide.

Lungs

When a person inhales, oxygen enters the body through the lungs. The body uses oxygen to turn fuel into energy.

THE BODY ON THE BOARD

Skateboarding is a full-body activity. It requires strength, coordination, and energy. Muscles, bones, and organs work together to flow smoothly from one movement to the next.

After a day of skateboarding, a skater may be sore. Soreness is a result of tiny tears in muscle tissue. Soreness usually goes away after a few days.

Muscles

Inside the muscles, cells turn oxygen and sugar into power. Muscles propel the body to run, jump, and skate.

Knees

By bending and straightening their knees, skaters transfer energy into their boards. This can help them get up a steep slope.

Feet

Feet form the foundation of balance. Shifting the body's weight from one foot to the other allows a skater to jump. Skaters steer by rocking the board from side to side.

SAFETY EQUIPMENT

When a skater falls, he hits the ground with more force than if he had been standing still. Safety gear helps skaters protect themselves.

▶ **HELMET:**
A skateboarding helmet is hard and smooth on the outside. It has thick foam on the inside. A helmet helps absorb the impact if the head hits the ground.

▶ **WRIST GUARDS:**
Wrist guards protect the joints that connect hands to arms. When people fall, they tend to put their hands out to catch themselves. As a result, bones in the wrists can snap, and tissues can tear.

▶ **ELBOW AND KNEE PADS:**
Protective pads guard skin from scrapes. Skaters often end up sliding long distances when they fall.

G-FORCE

Falling is caused by gravity. Gravity is the attraction between two objects that have mass. It is the force that keeps us grounded on the earth. The force of gravity is determined by the amount of mass an object has. Objects with more mass have more weight. That means the force of gravity on them is larger.

We feel the effects of gravity all the time. The amount of force we feel is measured in "gs." Most of the time we live in a state of 1 g. But when a skater's head hits the ground, his skull can experience 100 gs.

LEARNING TO FALL

At some point, nearly everyone who gets on a skateboard falls off it. Falls happen because of a property called **INERTIA**. Inertia is described in Newton's first law of motion. This law explains why a skater's body will keep on moving when his board stops.

NEWTON'S FIRST LAW OF MOTION:

A body at rest tends to stay at rest, unless acted on by an outside force. A body in motion tends to stay in motion and move in a straight line, unless acted on by an outside force.

INERTIA — an object's state in which the object stays at rest or keeps moving in the same direction until a force acts on the object

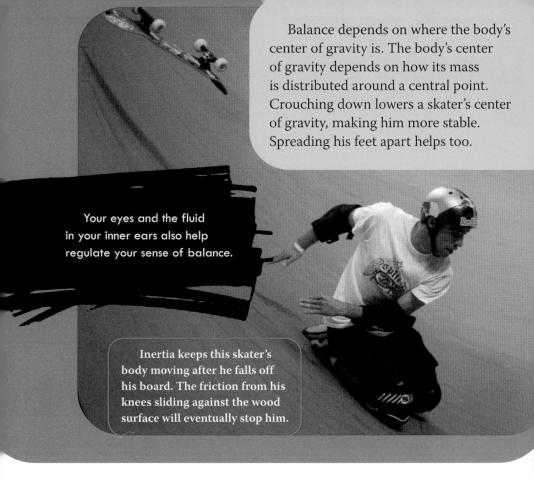

Balance depends on where the body's center of gravity is. The body's center of gravity depends on how its mass is distributed around a central point. Crouching down lowers a skater's center of gravity, making him more stable. Spreading his feet apart helps too.

Your eyes and the fluid in your inner ears also help regulate your sense of balance.

Inertia keeps this skater's body moving after he falls off his board. The friction from his knees sliding against the wood surface will eventually stop him.

One way to avoid injury is to learn how to fall properly. An experienced skater crouches down. Crouching lessens the distance of the fall and the gs of impact. He tries to land on his shoulder or back. Then he wraps his arms around his head and rolls. Rolling spreads out the energy of the fall over time and distance.

CHAPTER 2

▷ GET MOVING

Skateboarding is all about movement. It may seem simple, but movement is more complicated than you might think.

Isaac Newton figured out a few basic laws of motion in the late 1600s. We've already covered the laws of gravity and inertia. They help explain why skaters fall. The law of inertia also helps explain how skaters move.

The inertia of a moving skateboard propels this skater off the halfpipe and into the air. Gravity will eventually pull him back down.

NEWTON'S INSPIRATION

Newton wanted to explain why the moon moves around the earth and the planets move around the sun. He came up with the law of universal gravitation. All objects have gravity. The gravity of a more massive object attracts smaller objects to it. This force causes smaller objects to orbit around larger ones. It's also what keeps us firmly grounded on the earth. But smaller objects also pull larger ones toward them. The gravity of the moon pulls up ocean tides on the earth.

Since a body at rest will stay at rest, a skater standing still on a board will remain motionless. He needs an outside force to get him moving. He could push off with his foot to give the board a shove. He could also stand on top of a hill and lean. Gravity will roll him down the slope.

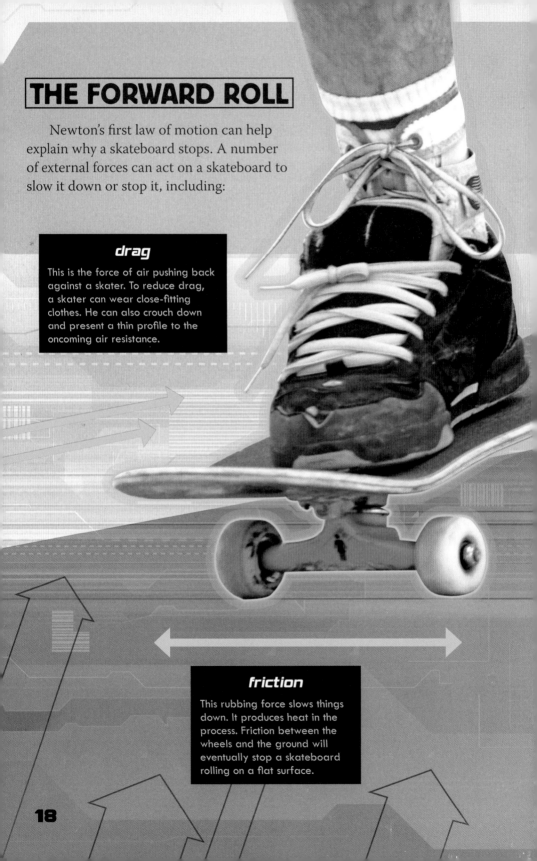

THE FORWARD ROLL

Newton's first law of motion can help explain why a skateboard stops. A number of external forces can act on a skateboard to slow it down or stop it, including:

drag

This is the force of air pushing back against a skater. To reduce drag, a skater can wear close-fitting clothes. He can also crouch down and present a thin profile to the oncoming air resistance.

friction

This rubbing force slows things down. It produces heat in the process. Friction between the wheels and the ground will eventually stop a skateboard rolling on a flat surface.

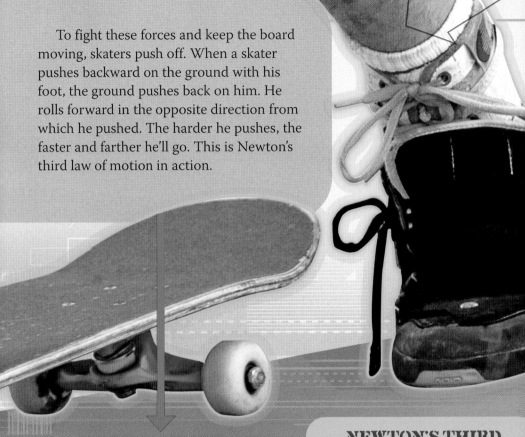

To fight these forces and keep the board moving, skaters push off. When a skater pushes backward on the ground with his foot, the ground pushes back on him. He rolls forward in the opposite direction from which he pushed. The harder he pushes, the faster and farther he'll go. This is Newton's third law of motion in action.

gravity

If a rolling board starts moving up an incline, gravity will pull it back down.

NEWTON'S THIRD LAW OF MOTION:
Every action has an equal and opposite reaction.

SKATEBOARDING TIME LINE

- **1950s:** California surfers start putting wheels on wooden boards.
- **1963:** First competitions take place.
- **1965:** First international skateboarding competition is held, including freestyle and slalom skateboarding.
- **1972:** Urethane wheels are invented.
- **1975:** The Zephyr team, made up of early professional skaters, shocks the world with their amazing tricks.
- **1976:** First skateparks are built.
- **1978:** Alan Gelfand invents the Ollie.
- **1980s:** Skateboarding videos give the public a glimpse of the sport and start influencing skateboarding style.
- **1995:** ESPN holds the first X Games, originally called the Extreme Games.

WORK IT

In skateboarding, any type of pushing, turning, or pulling motion requires work. Work is a force applied over distance.

kinetic energy

Energy is what allows people to do work. Energy also moves cars, lights up rooms, and boils water. Energy doesn't come out of thin air. There is a certain amount of energy that exists in the universe. Energy cannot be created or destroyed. This idea is known as the law of conservation of energy.

Energy can change forms. A skater standing at the top of an incline is full of potential energy. This is stored energy. It is waiting to be changed into kinetic energy.

potential energy

Kinetic energy is energy in motion. A skater traveling down an incline or doing a trick is loaded with kinetic energy.

When an athlete transforms potential energy to kinetic energy, some energy is lost in the form of heat. That's part of the reason why people get hot and sweaty when they exercise.

THE NEED FOR SPEED

Newton's second law of motion explains how a skater's weight affects his speed. This law is usually written as the equation F=MA. That stands for Force = Mass x Acceleration. Acceleration describes how quickly something speeds up or slows down.

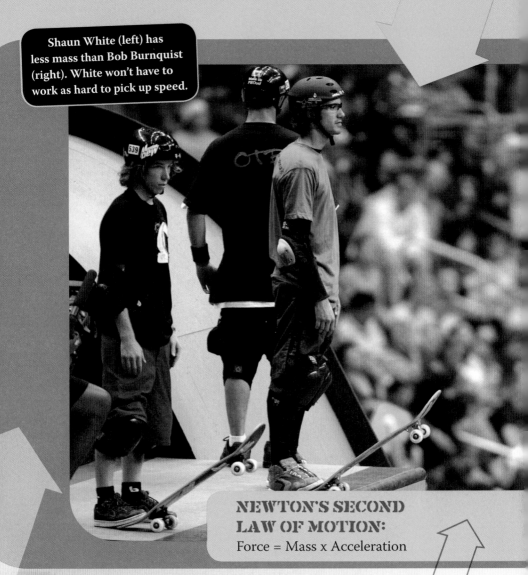

Shaun White (left) has less mass than Bob Burnquist (right). White won't have to work as hard to pick up speed.

NEWTON'S SECOND LAW OF MOTION:
Force = Mass x Acceleration

MASS, ACCELERATION, AND FORCE

Two skaters stand at the top of a hill. They start rolling at the same time. One skater is twice the size of the other skater. He has double the mass of the other skater. Because they are rolling down the same hill, the amount of acceleration is the same between the two skaters. But the actual force is equal to a skater's mass times acceleration. The larger skater will have double the force compared to that of the smaller skater.

The reason the smaller skater doesn't go as far is friction. Air friction is the main source of friction. It is the friction caused by the skaters moving through the air. Air friction is stronger against the larger skater, but not double the friction of the smaller skater. Because of this, the larger skater will end up rolling farther.

The more mass an object has, the more energy it takes to get that object moving. For example, a bowling ball and a beach ball are about the same size. But it's harder to push a heavy bowling ball than a lightweight beach ball.

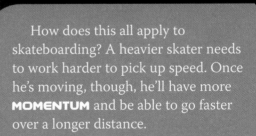

How does this all apply to skateboarding? A heavier skater needs to work harder to pick up speed. Once he's moving, though, he'll have more **MOMENTUM** and be able to go faster over a longer distance.

MOMENTUM — a property of a moving object equal to its mass times its velocity

TURN, TURN, TURN

Once an object is moving, it will tend to go in a straight line. Making an object move in a curved path requires a **CENTRIPETAL FORCE**. Twisting a long, straight object like a skateboard requires a special pair of forces called **TORQUE**.

One of the first things a new skater learns to do is turn. By leaning forward onto his toes, a skater tilts the edge of his board toward the ground.

▶ In an opposite way, the back edge underneath his heels lifts up slightly. This makes the board curve toward the toe edge.

▶ In an equal way, the more the skater leans, the more sharply he'll turn.

CENTRIPETAL FORCE — a force that pulls an object toward a center that it is rotating around

TORQUE — a pair of connected forces moving in opposite directions around a central point

CENTRIPETAL FLING

Attach an object to the end of a string. If you hold the end of the string and swing it around, the object will move in a perfect circle. The string provides the centripetal force to keep the object curving around.

What do you think will happen if you let go of the string in mid-swing? Will the object keep curving around, or will it move in a straight line?

The object will move in a straight line in whatever direction it was released. Then gravity will take over and pull it to the ground.

The rear wheel assembly is connected by an angled pin. This pin turns the wheels to the left. The combination of the front wheels turning right and the rear wheels turning left makes the skateboard carve a turn to the right.

The wheels and trucks make up the wheel assemblies of the skateboard. The front wheel assembly is connected to the board by an upward-angled pin. This angle is the key to all skateboard motion. When you shift your weight to the right side of the skateboard this pin causes the assembly to swing. As a result, both front wheels make a right turn.

CHAPTER 3

STREET SKATING AND BASIC TRICKS

You've got the basic laws of physics under your belt. Now you can begin to understand how skaters perform some of their tricks.

OLLIE UP

One popular trick is called the Ollie. To pop an Ollie, a skater leaps off the ground with the board seemingly glued to his feet. An Ollie allows a skater to hop over obstacles and onto curbs and rails.

1

2

The skater starts with bent knees. This lowers his center of gravity. He shifts his weight to his back foot. This shift pushes the kicktail down, which makes the nose lift up.

The nose lifts up and gains upward speed. As the skater straightens his legs and raises his arms, the board launches upward.

Danny Wainwright set the record for the highest Ollie performed on flat ground. He reached a height of 44.5 inches (113 centimeters).

5

Gravity pulls the board and the skater down. The skater lands and rolls on.

4

3

The skater pushes down with his front foot. He lifts his back foot. This slides the board into a flat position in midair.

In the air, the skater slides his front foot forward. The friction between the foot and the grip tape pulls the board up higher.

THE NEXT LEVEL

An advanced skater can do some pretty amazing tricks once he is in the air. Spins are especially impressive. They are measured in degrees of a circle. A full circle is made up of 360 degrees. A quarter turn is 90 degrees. A half turn is 180 degrees. A spin and a half equals 540 degrees.

90 degrees

180 degrees

360 degrees

THE LAW OF CONSERVATION OF ANGULAR MOMENTUM:

An object will rotate only if acted on by an outside force. It will keep rotating unless acted on by an outside force. Midair rotations appear to break this law because the only force around is gravity. Gravity alone can't get an object spinning.

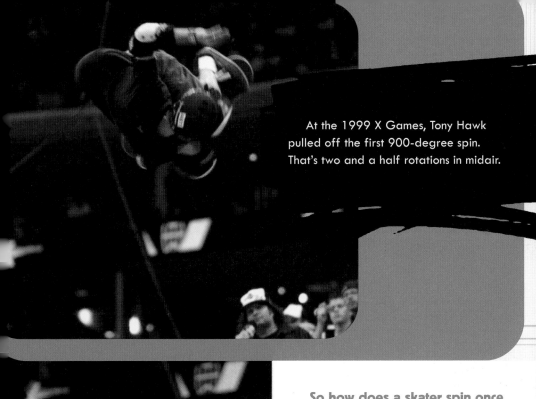

At the 1999 X Games, Tony Hawk pulled off the first 900-degree spin. That's two and a half rotations in midair.

So how does a skater spin once he's in the air? Try this activity to find out.

▶ Stand still. Then jump straight up. Once you're in the air, spin as far as you can. As you spin, pay attention to what your arms, hips, and legs are doing.

▶ Your legs twisted one way while your arms twisted the other.

▶ Because your legs balance the motion of your arms, angular momentum is conserved.

▶ Skaters do the same thing to generate spinning motion once airborne.

SKATEPARKS

A skatepark is like a playground for skaters. Most parks include sloped surfaces, jumps, stairs, and rails.

stairs

jumps

sloped surface

rails

Skaters swarm to some parks. Other parks are like ghost towns. Designers want to create parks that bring skaters back again and again. To be successful, they must create a park that is challenging but not too challenging. The layout should be fun for a range of experience levels.

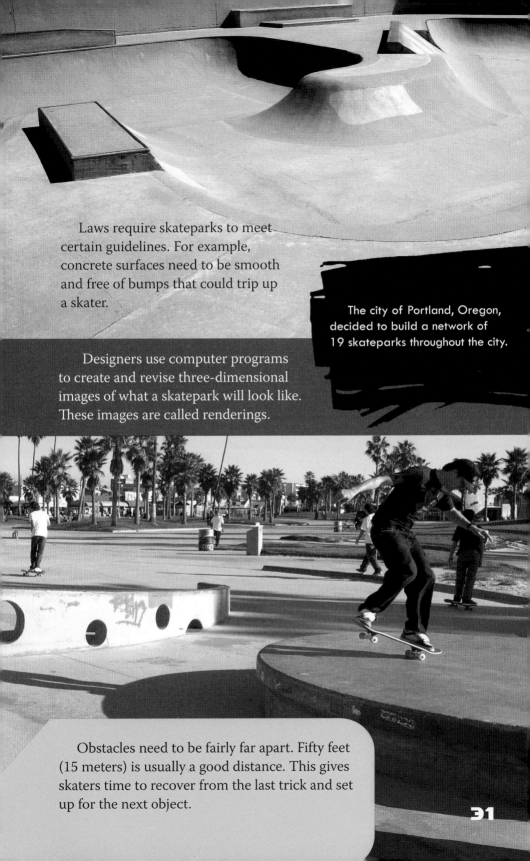

Laws require skateparks to meet certain guidelines. For example, concrete surfaces need to be smooth and free of bumps that could trip up a skater.

The city of Portland, Oregon, decided to build a network of 19 skateparks throughout the city.

Designers use computer programs to create and revise three-dimensional images of what a skatepark will look like. These images are called renderings.

Obstacles need to be fairly far apart. Fifty feet (15 meters) is usually a good distance. This gives skaters time to recover from the last trick and set up for the next object.

IN THE SWIM

The first skaters were surfers who wanted something to do when there were no waves. Some early skaters got big thrills in empty swimming pools. Skating in pools is illegal. But there were no skateparks in the 1960s. Pools gave skaters their first opportunities to go vertical.

In a swimming pool, there is usually some flat ground at the bottom between steep walls. The curved area between the flat surface and the wall is called a transition. The transition is like an arc of a circle. If you were to draw the rest of the circle, you could measure its **RADIUS**.

RADIUS — the distance from an outside point of a circle to the circle's center; a radius is half of a circle's diameter.

The bowl-shaped obstacles found at skateparks were inspired by swimming pools from the 1960s.

The bigger the radius, the more gradual the transition is. If a transition is too small, a skater will slam into the wall.

An ideal transition radius should measure 4 to 6 feet (1.2 to 1.8 meters). At the very least, a transition's radius should be as big as the distance from the ground to a skater's belly button. Then his body can naturally pivot around his center of gravity.

HALFPIPE AND VERT SKATING

Skaters who seek the highest air and the biggest tricks skate on ramps. Two ramps facing each other are called a halfpipe.

In the beginning, halfpipes looked like what they sound like — round pipes with the top half sawed off. Today's halfpipes have a longer flat area between the two sloping sides. This transition area gives the skater a little more time to prepare for the next trick.

Ramps are also called quarterpipes. They range in size from 2-foot (.6-meter) micro-ramps to 16-foot (5-meter) professional vert ramps. A typical ramp is 16 feet (5 meters) wide.

professional vert ramp
16 feet tall

wall

BALANCING ENERGY

Skating in a halfpipe demonstrates the balance between potential energy and kinetic energy. When a skater stands at the top of the pipe, his potential energy is at a maximum. Because he is high up, gravity will transform potential energy into kinetic energy when he drops into the pipe. Then the skater skates back up the other side of the pipe. As he does this, he loses kinetic energy and slows down. Once he reaches the top, he is again full of potential energy and can drop back in again.

Plywood and steel are common materials for the base of a ramp. The surface should be ultra-smooth. A smooth surface minimizes friction, allowing higher speeds. Seams and screws that stick out can cause painful wipeouts.

Some companies make materials that minimize injuries from wipeouts. These materials are strong, smooth, and easy to repair or replace.

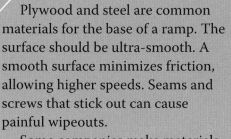

transition area

wall →

PUMP YOU UP

In halfpipes and skateparks, skaters often cruise from one ramp to another without ever putting a foot down to push. How does a skater fight the forces of gravity and friction, maintain speed, and stay on his board? The secret is pumping.

As a skater rolls down a transition, he crouches to lower his center of gravity. Doing this lightens the force on the board. The skater stands as he moves up the other side of the pipe. This raises his center of gravity and adds pressure to the board. It also adds energy and speed to the skater's uphill motion.

Pumping also helps a skater keep moving in a kidney-shaped bowl. Over every bump, he crouches and stands up again. He gets an extra dose of energy with every pump.

center of gravity

Skaters can pump and carve turns at the same time. They pump on the board while alternating their body weight between toeside and heelside. With this motion, a skater can accelerate with each turn.

On a 16-foot (5-meter) professional ramp, a skater usually reaches about 22 miles (35 kilometers) per hour. On a 6-foot (2-meter) mini-ramp, skaters can speed to 15 miles (24 kilometers) per hour.

At the highest point of an aerial trick, a skater is full of potential energy. Gravity converts the potential energy to kinetic energy, bringing the skater back down.

The faster a skater goes down the pipe, the more momentum he'll have going back up. With more momentum, he'll get higher in the air.

SPEED AND SIZE

A heavier skater needs to work harder and use more energy to go as fast as a lighter skater does. If both skaters get up to the same top speeds, they'll reach the same height. However, it is easier for lighter skaters to go faster, so they tend to reach greater heights. Lighter skaters are also less likely to get injured in a fall. That's because there's less energy involved.

Danny Way jumped over the Great Wall of China five times in one day.

WAY COOL

Californian Danny Way is on a mission to break world records on his skateboard. He holds the records for both the longest and highest jumps. The longest jump was 79 feet (24 meters). The highest jump was 23.5 feet (7 meters). In July 2005, he leaped over the Great Wall of China. On his final Wall jump, he pulled a 360 in midair. Way also set the official world speed record on a skateboard at 74 miles (119 kilometers) per hour. He held onto a rope and was pulled by a car.

COMPETITIONS

Local skateparks host their own small contests. Competitions also happen on the state, national, and international levels.

The two main categories in skateboarding competitions are street and vert skating. There may also be slalom, freestyle, and big air competitions. Men compete separately from women. Sometimes skaters split into age groups.

In vert competitions, skaters build up speed as they skate back and forth in the halfpipe. Once they have enough momentum, they fly into the air and perform crazy tricks.

In slalom competitions, skaters pump while carving turns around obstacles.

In the street category, skaters do tricks off obstacles. These obstacles include stairs, rails, and ramps.

Judges usually score skaters on a series of attempts. Depending on the category, points are awarded for height, style, speed, and creativity. The skater with the highest score wins!

SWEAT IT OUT

Skateboarding is work, and work requires energy. When the body does work, some of its energy is released as heat. Once the body heats up enough, the brain tells it to sweat. Sweating is the body's own cooling system. When sweat evaporates off a person's skin, it cools down the body. But too much sweating can be dangerous. When someone loses too much fluid, the body doesn't perform its best. Low fluid levels can make a person very sick. That's why skaters keep the fluids flowing!

BEST OF THE BEST

The best skaters work their way up to major competitions. These include the X Games and the Dew Tour.

BIG AIR

In the X Games Big Air competition, skaters fly down an 80-foot (24-meter) ramp. They reach speeds near 40 miles (64 kilometers) per hour. From there, they launch over a 70-foot (21-meter) gap. In the air, they may spin, flip, or do both. Skaters land and finish on a 27-foot (8-meter) ramp. There skaters pull a final trick. They can get up to 50 feet (15 meters) off the ground.

27 feet

Skaters are endlessly creative when it comes to trying new things. Some crazy skateboarding feats include:

▶ **Longest distance covered in a 24-hour period**
In 2008, Ted McDonald traveled 242 miles (389.5 kilometers) on his skateboard in one day.

▶ **Most Ollies performed in a row in a halfpipe**
In 2007, Rob Dyrdek pulled off 46 Ollies in a row.

▶ **Longest free fall**
In 2008, Danny Way and his skateboard dropped 28 feet (8.5 meters) off a giant guitar at the Hard Rock Cafe in Las Vegas, Nevada.

EAT THIS

According to the law of conservation of energy, we cannot create energy. So where do skaters get energy to perform their tricks? Food! When people eat, they take in chemical energy. The body stores this energy as carbohydrates, protein, and fat. When a skater hops on his board, his cells change these substances into energy. Energy from food is measured in Calories. If a person who weighed 150 pounds (68 kilograms) skateboarded for one hour, he would burn about 340 Calories.

WHERE TO NEXT?

Skateboarding hasn't been around that long. The sport attracts more and more people each year. Skaters are sure to invent new tricks, race to higher speeds, and soar to new heights.

In the popular 1980s movie *Back to the Future II*, the main character rides a hoverboard. This futuristic skateboard floats through the air, just above the ground. Since the 1980s, people have actually made some flying boards. They use engines to stay afloat. But most of these boards are heavy, noisy, and slow. Maybe someday, someone will invent a better-performing hoverboard.

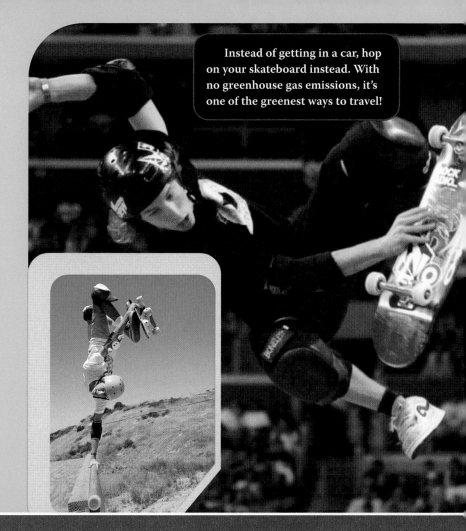

Instead of getting in a car, hop on your skateboard instead. With no greenhouse gas emissions, it's one of the greenest ways to travel!

GREEN SKATEBOARDING

Skateboarding has left its mark on the earth. Trees are cut down to provide wood for boards. Ramp surfaces and skateboard decks and wheels end up in landfills. Skateparks replace grassy parks.

Some skaters and skateboard companies are working to make the sport "greener." Eco-friendly strategies include:

- making skateboard decks out of recycled wood or from trees that grow back quickly, such as bamboo, birch, and poplar
- making grip tape out of recycled glass bottles
- decorating boards with inks that are made with a water base instead of harsh chemicals
- making boards that are lighter and use less wood
- reusing and recycling waste materials created during production
- sealing decks with nontoxic glues

45

GLOSSARY

centripetal force (sen-TRI-puh-tuhl FORS) — the force that pulls an object turning in a circle inward toward the center

diameter (dye-AM-uh-tur) — the length of a straight line through the center of a circle

drag (DRAG) — the force created when air strikes a moving object; drag slows down moving objects.

friction (FRIK-shuhn) — a force created when two objects rub together; friction slows down objects.

fulcrum (FUL-kruhm) — the point on which a lever rests

gravity (GRAV-uh-tee) — a force that pulls objects together

inertia (in-UR-shuh) — an object's state in which the object stays at rest or keeps moving until a force acts on the object

kinetic energy (ki-NET-ik EN-ur-jee) — the energy of a moving object

momentum (moh-MEN-tuhm) — a property of a moving object equal to its mass times its velocity

potential energy (puh-TEN-shuhl EN-ur-jee) — the stored energy of an object that is raised, stretched, or squeezed

radius (RAY-dee-uhss) — a straight line segment drawn from the center of a circle to its outer edge

torque (TORK) — a pair of connected forces moving in opposite directions around a central point

truck (TRUHK) — a piece on the bottom of the deck that holds the wheels on a skateboard

READ MORE

Becker, Helaine. *Skateboarding Science.* Sports Science. New York: Crabtree, 2009.

Fridell, Ron. *Sports Technology.* Cool Science. Minneapolis: Lerner, 2009.

Hasan, Heather. *Skateboarding Today and Tomorrow.* Super Skateboarding. New York: Rosen, 2009.

Stock, Charlotte, and Ben Powell. *Skateboarding Step-By-Step.* Skills in Motion. New York: Rosen, 2010.

INTERNET SITES

FactHound offers a safe, fun way to find Internet sites related to this book. All of the sites on Facthound have been researched by our staff.

Here's all you do:

Visit *www.facthound.com*

FactHound will fetch the best sites for you!

INDEX